# CAMBRIDGE TRAVEL GUIDE

How to have the best day out in Cambridge, explore the hidden gems and discover local secrets.

Sarah Glover

*To Megan and Hannah who continually inspire me.*

# CONTENTS

# WELCOME TO MY GUIDEBOOK
## of Cambridge

Enclosed in this book is a walking path that will take you on a journey of discovery where you will experience the true essence of Cambridge. It will allow you to marvel at the astonishing architecture and the remarkable history of the people who live and have lived here. The tour you embark on is just under a mile long which would only take 16 minutes if walked non-stop. It begins at The Fitzwilliam Museum on Trumpington Street and continues along Kings Parade, a stunning thoroughfare through the city and ends with a relaxing and informative punt where you will see features of the city you can appreciate no other way.

SARAH GLOVER

# ABOUT THE PHOTOGRAPHER

The photos in this book have been taken by Vanessa Champion (Ness). She has kindly provided a link where prints of these photos can be purchased and sent to your home to help you create forever memories.

Based in the UK, Ness was originally planning on coming to St John's in Cambridge to study Classics, but in the end, started her professional career as an academic at University College London with a PhD in Greek and Latin and working in the British Museum. During her academic career, she started taking commercial and portrait photographs which have grown into stand-alone ventures including PhotoAid Global Foundation. Ness established her publication, The Journal of Biophilic Design, a magazine and international podcast series. Passionate about our natural world, she is the founder of Virtual Nature Walls which publishes small and large-scale virtual nature views for residential and commercial interiors. Link here for photos.https://6647440.tifmember.com/p/81477gms/30030587705/architecture-bridge-sighs-

SARAH GLOVER

# cambridge

# INTRODUCTION

The spectacles of this city, the history and the architecture are vast; it would be impossible to put everything to see and do in one small book. However, here, I have selected the iconic sites locals and internationals adore and have provided an interactive tour with links and keywords to search for further reading. This way you can get a true understanding of the history and the people who live and work here.

# LOCAL PEOPLE

The local people are thoughtful and many are very intelligent. They will be kind and answer your questions. However, be prepared for the long answer and don't be surprised to find you are talking to a Nobel prize winner or a famous IT technician. Cambridge has produced well over one hundred Nobel laureates since 1904. I have added places to never be forgotten and experiences which will inspire and astonish you. It is entirely possible to become transfixed with the quintessential views of this historical city.

In the very early morning throughout the year, it's possible to see smoking mist drifting silently along the river. In the winter there is the sharp cold silver frost which lays along the branches of the trees making them look like spectacular natural architecture. Cambridge is an incredible place to be. Practise your photography skills amongst a plethora of historical buildings and people from all over the globe; history meets today in a truly international style.

# PRE-TRIP PLANNING

Use a search engine to get up-to-the-minute information on opening times and important news. At the end of this book, there are some search engine-friendly headings for you to use as a framework for reference. In addition, I have included some fun and informative links for outings to suit families and individual preferences. With this ever-changing world, I suggest combining this book with the most up-to-date data, current prices and booking information. Search out the magnificent opportunities there are to discover and enjoy the treasures and stories of Cambridge.

# PRE-TRIP MOVIE WATCHING

Listed below are some charming movies which feature Cambridge and are thoroughly recommended to watch while packing to get you in the mood for the city and give you an overall sense of the history of the city.

The Theory of Everything 2014 - A story of the life of Stephen Hawking

The Man Who Knows Infinity 2015 - Biographical drama about mathematician Srinivasa Ramanujan

The History Boys 2006 - Coming of age

Sylvia 2003 - The story of Silvia Plath played by Gwyneth Paltrow.

# WHAT TO EXPECT

# Cyclists

Cambridge is the city of bikes. That is probably the first thing to know. It is important to learn how to navigate the shared pavements and pathways. Cyclists should give way to pedestrians, nevertheless, be prepared to jump out of the way should one veer towards you. Cycle lanes are usually indicated by a bicycle painted on the pathway or a signpost close to the road. Do stay out of their way as much as possible as cyclists can speed along very fast.

## Bike Hire

Cambridge has more than 85 miles of cycle lanes and 1 in 4 people cycle to work. Cycling is the main form of transport for most of the people who live and study here. A cyclist counting machine was installed in 2014 to mark Cambridge's contribution to the Tour de France visit. It is situated on Gonville Place by the side of the Parkers Piece and in December of 2016, the number of cyclists passing by exceeded one million.

## Bicycle rental

It is possible to hire a bike from the Cambridge Main station or use a search engine to find other companies online and contact them in advance. Rutland Cycling has great reviews. Bike hire is busy, can be hectic and you may need to book ahead of time. It is recommended you wear a bike helmet as they can save your life if you fall off or get into an accident. In addition, the company Cambridge Bike Tours provides an entertaining tour taking in many of the sites.

## The Great British Weather

The British are famous globally for the never-ending discussion of the weather. The reason behind this is that it is so changeable! England, one of the four nations of the United Kingdom, is next to The Atlantic Ocean and mainland Europe, with six air masses converging at various times throughout the year from such diverse places as the Arctic and Africa. Our weather varies with the 'wind' as the year passes through the seasons. Be prepared for anything and bring an umbrella or be ready to buy one (from almost every store in the city) if a downpour greets you.

# WHAT TO WEAR

## Comfortable shoes

Cambridge is flat, with an average elevation of only 47 feet (14 metres) above sea level; you can walk just about everywhere. Castle Mound is an excellent place to take a picnic to watch the May Ball, November fireworks or the sunrise or sunset. Find Castle Mound by walking out of the city on Bridge Street, over Magdalene Bridge and up the hill. Turn right into the car park and you will see the grassy hill that is Castle Mound.

## Layers

Bring clothing layers so you can easily switch from cool to warm with the weather and always do a local weather check each day before heading out to confirm the temperature. Smart-casual comfortable clothes will take you anywhere and are what most locals wear.

# WHERE TO STAY

## Airbnb

Airbnb is a great addition to the many hotels in Cambridge. Pricing varies between £35 - £500 or more per night. However, a couple of tips for when choosing where to stay, consider not only your budget but the distance and transport or walking route to the city centre. For example, a 30-minute walk along the River Cam is truly delightful, but a walk in and out of busy streets may not be so interesting. Get the postcode and search on maps to confirm where your accommodation is located. There is a fabulous recommended one-bed apartment, (pictured above) overlooking the River Cam with a 30-minute walk along the river to the city centre.

https://airbnb.com/h/

lightsunnyspaciousriverviewrowersswanstreessunriseandsunse
tsmoonlightonthewater

## Hotels

There are many good hotels in the town.

The Fellows House and Madingley Hall are two such hotels. One for the architecture and the latter for the soft luxurious bed sheets.

The Gonville Hotel can be expensive, however, it is in the town centre and it is easy to walk everywhere.

The Varsity Hotel has a spa and gym and is right in the city. In summer it is a favourite place to watch the sun go down while sipping a cocktail at the rooftop bar.

The Premier Inn is a short walk into town along a busy road but can be a good value for money.

# GETTING AROUND

## Buses

Buses in the UK are usually reliable, safe and easy to use. Some bus stops have computerised tracking so you know almost exactly how long it will be until the next bus comes along. As always, planning your route, finding the bus stop, and getting the ticket before travel can help you have an enjoyable time and reduce stress no end. Buy your tickets and find the bus timetable online at; www.stagecoachbus.com/plan-a-journey. There are also hop-on-hop-off sightseeing tour buses, seen in many cities in the UK and further afield.

## Trains

The train system is clean and the trains usually run on time. In Cambridge, there are two stations both within walking distance of the city. Cambridge Main Station, and Cambridge North. These stations have fast links to London, Gatwick, and Stansted airports and provide services to the East to Birmingham and the seaside in Norfolk. Below is a website address and link to help you plan your travel. If tickets are booked early there are often discounts available. https://www.thetrainline.com/destinations/trains-to-cambridge

## E-bikes and scooters

E-bikes and scooters can be found on street corners all over the city. Download the Voi app onto your phone to get started. https://www.voiscooters.comhttps://www.voiscooters.com

# A BRIEF OVERVIEW OF THE
# HISTORY OF THE CITY

There have been settlements in Cambridge since the Bronze Age, 4000 years ago. The Romans settled here and built a fort on Castle Hill in the first century. However, as the Roman Empire declined in the fifth century, the castle was abandoned. Cambridge was originally called Granta Brygg and was renamed later as the town grew. An entry in the Doomsday book in 1086 records a population of 31 households. After this, Cambridge went through many trials of being captured, burned to the ground, and hit by plagues. By the thirteenth century, there were weekly markets and a fair where people from all over would come to buy and sell goods. Midsummer Fair was born at this time and apart from a brief pause during the World Wars and the 2020 Covid pandemic, it still runs today.

Despite the fact it does not have a cathedral, Cambridge was granted city status in 1951 in recognition of its history and economic and administrative contributions to the lawful government of the United Kingdom.

# CAMBRIDGE UNIVERSITY

One of the most prestigious universities in the world, Cambridge University was founded in 1209. It is made up of 31 colleges which are dotted around the city.

Peterhouse, the oldest college, was founded in 1284 and the most recent to be founded were Lucy Cavendish College and Clare Hall which were both established in 1965.

Two shameful facts are that women were not admitted into the colleges until 1869 when the first women's college of Girton was established 2.5 miles out of the city. Cambridge was the last of the well-known education facilities to award women their degrees and did not do so until 1948.

## King's College

King's College and the chapel with its exceptional architecture are found on King's Parade in the heart of the city centre. Inside the immense chapel, you will find world-class fan vaulted ceilings. King's College is recognised for its recording of the Christmas Eve carol service which began in 1918 and has been broadcasted on the radio since 1928. For some families, listening to Carols from King's is now a tradition that many tune into while stirring the Christmas pudding and preparing for Christmas day. The carols which always begin with Once in Royal David's City are sung by the world-famous King's College

Choir.

On Christmas Day, if you queue early enough it may be possible to be allowed into the candlelit space of the Chapel. Here the sense of history blends with the fragrance of Frankincense and the angelic voices of the choir. It is alleged that if you close your eyes while listening to the choir on Christmas day, you will be transported to heaven.

## Trinity College

Walking north along Kings Parade, the road turns into Trinity Street, where Trinity College Great Gate protects the entrance to the college.

Sir Issac Newton studied here and on the lawn outside Trinity College, you will see an apple tree said to be a graft from the original tree where Newton first saw the apple drop to the ground and his concept of gravity was born. Folklore tells us that while he was studying at Trinity College his room was one of the ones which overlooked the front lawn where the apple tree now grows. Trinity Street changes into St John's Street and as it does so you will find St John's College.

# St John's College

St John's College was founded by Henry VI's mother, Lady Margaret Beaufort, in 1511. As with all the colleges in Cambridge, St John's has an impressive list of alumni which adds to its glory and prestige; including William Wordsworth and William Wilberforce and to date, a total of ten Nobel prize winners.

# THE FITZWILLIAM MUSEUM

Built in 1848 by George Basev in a neoclassical style. The Fitzwilliam was completed by Charles Cockerell after Basev died in 1845. The Fitzwilliam museum is free to enter and is full of inordinate treasures. There are family events and discovery classes and paid-for tours available all week. As you walk up the steps to the entrance to the museum, look up. In England, it is a good practice to look at the roofs and tops of the buildings as they can be spectacular.

# THE MARKET

Cambridge has had a market since the Middle Ages and you will find it in the town square every day. On Saturday there are often over 100 stalls where you will find food, plants, bread, clothes, coffee, cakes, and cheeses. It is a noisy and friendly place to buy memorabilia, lunch and snacks and Cambridge branded goods. As you wander in and out of the stalls the chatter of people speaking varied and distant languages combined with the smell of exotic spices and a hint of rose and Jasmine from the flower stall altogether gives an international flavour.

# Pubs

Pubs are a tradition in the UK that is believed to have started in Roman times with the opening of tavernas to serve wine to the legions of Roman soldiers. The name changed to taverns and Inns and public houses opened which began to include food, accommodation, and the locals' favourite drinks. These names amalgamated together and were shortened to pubs. One of the oldest pubs in England is in Nottingham and is dated 1189 AD. Today in Cambridge you will find countless pubs serving delicious food.

The Fort St George located on the river is a favourite of the locals and visitors to the city. It is also occasionally frequented by the Duke and Duchess of Cambridge.

## The Eagle

The Eagle is a busy, bustling pub, in the centre of town. Crick and Watson, the famous geneticists, announced the discovery of the DNA Double Helix in 1953.

The RAF Bar ceiling

The RAF Bar

At the Eagle, you will also find The RAF bar, where pilots from all over the world and some from WWII signed the ceiling to be remembered forever. There is more than enough fascinating memorabilia here to keep you engrossed for a good couple of hours.

# FOOD

## Lunch

There are countless places to eat lunch in the city and it's possible to walk into most restaurants and ask for a table. However, on a busy summer weekend particularly during university graduations, it is worth booking in advance. Steak & Honour and Doppelganger each serve fast, delicious burgers. Bills and The Pint shop are great for tasty wholesome food.

## Michelin Starred food

Midsummer House for a fancy lunch or special event. The two-star Michelin restaurant will delight you with delicious flavours and seasonal ingredients. From town, it is a 10–15-minute walk through the parks to Midsummer Common and along the River Cam, it is situated next to The Fort St George pub.

MJP@The Shepherds - At the time of writing it does not yet have a Michelin Star however, rumour has it will have one soon, so head along and enjoy the tasty food at pre-star prices! It is located just outside Cambridge in Fen Ditton, a lovely pub worth the 15-minute taxi ride or a cycle ride over the Abbey-Chesterton bridge and through the commons.

## Cakes and Chelsea buns

Fitzbillies Chelsea buns, a Cambridge tradition begun in 1920 by two brothers. Their father Tucker Mason had a shop on Trumpington Street baking bread, so they decided to make cakes and Chelsea buns. Fitzbillies start baking every day at 4 am except for Christmas and New Year's Day. On a busy day, over 800 buns are eaten. This is a great place to buy your picnic to take when you go punting.

## Fudge

Watch fudge being made and get a free sample at the Fudge Kitchen on King's Parade opposite the entrance to King's College.

# Afternoon Tea

The most quintessential British pastime if there ever was one.

In the 1800s, the 17th Duchess of Bedford, Anna Maria Russell, a lifetime friend of Queen Victoria, began the tradition of having tea and cake at 4 pm each afternoon. As she invited her friends to join her; tea at 4 pm became an established British tradition.

Enjoy delicious small dainty sandwiches and freshly baked cake at Parker's Tavern, The Varsity Hotel, and Brown's Brasserie, all within walking distance of town, and all provide delicious assortments. In the summer The Orchard Tea Rooms, in Grantchester, is worth the taxi fare or cycling through Lammas Land.

# ONTO THE RIVER

The River Cam is a delightful spot for punting, and paddleboarding. There are 26 bridges along its length and walking along the towpaths you will see amongst other things, cows grazing on the commons, swans, and houseboats. The river is an important part of Cambridge life, there have been rowing races and seasonal events on it or close by since the Middle Ages.

The river is 155km long and divides loosely into Upper, Middle, and Lower rivers; it spans the counties of Hertfordshire, Essex, and Cambridgeshire. The river finishes its course by pouring into The River Great Ouse at Ely and flows out towards The Wash and The North Sea at Kings Lynn. The stretch of river that flows through Cambridge has been immortalised in poems, paintings, and stories. Find some of them in Geoffrey Chaucer's Canterbury Tales, The Reeve's Tale, and The Old Vicarage, Grantchester.

# PUNTING, THE BACKS, BRIDGES
# AND COLLEGES

Punting is a must to see the best Cambridge has to offer. For access to the nine bridges along the Backs, you must either enter the colleges (which are not always open to the public and often charge a fee) or go on a punting tour of "The Backs". However, you can see Magdalene bridge, Silver Street bridge, Garret Hostel, Clare, and the Mathematical bridge from the town.

Punting became popular in the early 20<sup>th</sup> century. Flat-bottomed boats glide effortlessly on the shallow waters of the River Cam. The punts are propelled along with a long pole dropped onto the riverbed and pushed off. It is a great skill and easily learnt. It is possible to hire your punt or have a guided tour where you can take a picnic to enjoy while your chauffeur reveals interesting historical stories of the University and life along the Cam. Local students often chauffeur the tours so you will be very well informed. Depending upon the tour you take, it may go under nine of the bridges discussed below and pass by eight of the 31 colleges and three libraries.

# Magdalene Bridge

Magdalene is also known to locals as the Great Bridge. It was the site where the first river crossing and bridge were built over the river Cam. It is pronounced Mord-lin bridge. Initially made out of wood in Roman times and was once the site of a ducking stool, it linked the North and South London trade routes. The original wooden bridge continually fell into disrepair and finally in the Spring of 1823 an iron bridge double the size of the original wooden bridge was designed. Arthur Browne was the architect, and the engineer was Benjamin Brown; its total cost was about £2,350.

## The Bridge of Sighs

The Bridge of Sighs is named after the Bridge of Sighs in Venice, Italy. In Venice, the bridge links the palace and the prison. However, in the UK it is part of St John's College and is one of the most photographed bridges in Cambridge. It links St John's College to the West side of the city. This area is known locally as the 'Backs' of Cambridge. The bridge is built in a Victorian Gothic Style and was designed by Henry Hutchinson in 1827. Originally it was named the 'New Bridge' and was built 9 years after the Mord-Lin iron bridge. It has appeared in films and paintings and was made famous by Lord Byron in his book Childe Harold's Pilgrimage. In 1963 it had a car suspended underneath by students' in an elaborate prank and it was featured in the movie The Theory of Everything. Even though the bridge is not open to the public and can be viewed while punting along the River Cam or from the Wren bridge when visiting the college.

## Mathematical Bridge

This bridge belongs to Queens College. It was designed by William Etheridge and built by James Essex in 1749. Since then, it has been repaired and rebuilt twice due to weathering of the original oak. The framework used is the tangent and radial trussing. There are two popular myths about this bridge, one was held together without any fixings and students took it apart to discover how it held together and could not put it back without bolts. The other is that it was designed and built by Sir Issac Newton. William Etheridge was a student of Issac Newton, which is where the myth may have originated.

## Trinity Bridge

Trinity College is the largest and wealthiest of all the colleges in Cambridge. One of the last acts of Henry VIII was founding Trinity College by combining the existing colleges Michaelhouse and Kings Hall. King Edwards Gate, which houses the Trinity College Clock, has been ticking since 1910. Many of the bridges in Cambridge were destroyed during the civil war in 1643. Trinity is one of those pulled down by Cromwell's men and reconstructed from stone; the bridge you see today was constructed by James Essex. Trinity bridge is one of the oldest, standing for almost 500 years.

## King's College Bridge

King College Bridge is a segmental arch Bridge, designed in 1820 by William Wilkins and built by Francis Braidwood. It is a simple addition to the remarkable King's College. Old English folk law has said the field opposite is the last place where duels were legally allowed to be held in England.

## The Kitchen Bridge or Wren Bridge at St John's

The Kitchen Bridge or Wren Bridge at St John's is the oldest bridge on the river Cam, named because the kitchens used to be on the opposite side of the river (on The Backs). The bridge is carved from a single block of limestone and was designed by Sir Christopher Wren. While you are punting, it is possible to see the watermarks on the cutwaters of the bridge from historical floods.

# Clare College Bridge

Clare College bridge is the oldest standing bridge on the Backs and was built by Thomas Grumbold in Ketton stone in 1639. There is a wedge missing from one of the stone finials; history tells us it is because the price for constructing the bridge was not paid in full and the stone mansion took a slice out of the ball to show his disgust at the lack of payment.

## Garrett Lane Hostel Bridge

Garrett Lane Hostel was built in 1960 and has interesting local names given to it by students. The huge effort by cyclists' to reach the top often results in various noises and exclamations of yes yes yes! It is a public right of way across the river made of a post-tensioned concrete bridge and designed by a student Timothy Morgan who sadly died before the bridge's completion. It is a great place for photos as it has a wonderful view of Clare Bridge.

## Bridge Jumping

Bridge jumping or hopping is a sport some students cannot resist, and they make it look easy! However, we do not recommend you try it! Here is how it's done. Climb from a punt onto the bridge above, send your punt under the bridge and then climb back down onto the punt on the other side whilst trying not to fall into the river.

SARAH GLOVER

## The Corpus Clock

The Corpus Clock was Invented, designed, and donated to Corpus Christi College by an alumnus, Dr John C Taylor OBE. It was installed in 2008 and is known locally as the time-eater clock.

It is a Chronophage displayed on the corner of Kings Parade and Benet Street in the doorway of the old NatWest Bank, now the exterior of the college library. A stunning feat of engineering, it has no numbers or hands, and the time is told by three rings of LED lights. The outermost ring of lights is the seconds passing, the middle the minutes and the smallest inside ring of lights tells the hour. At the thirty-second mark, the Chronophage will open its mouth and then snap it shut when the minute is over. On the hour chains will shake and a hammer will slam down onto a wooden coffin. Confirming that time is passing, and we will all die! If you can read Latin, you will see the inscription Mundus transit et concupiscentia eius, translated as 'the world and its desires pass away'. The clock is said to have a set of 50 tricks and if you look at it on the 25th of March or November, New Year's Day or Corpus Christi Day you will see some of them, keep your eyes peeled!

# CHURCHES

Cambridge has a long Christian heritage where it is believed to have had churches before the 10$^{th}$ century. Now there are approximately 40 and they cater to all denominations. They offer a warm welcome and magnificent stained-glass windows depicting stories of the gospels, great kings, and queens await all who visit.

## The Round Church

The Round Church was built in a Gothic style. Historians believe it was built around 1131. It is located diagonally opposite St John's College and is full of interesting history.

## The Church of St Benet

The Church of St Benet is where people have worshipped for over a thousand years and was believed to have been built in 1020. Until the 1600's students were called to lectures by the bells. Each Friday there are practice bell ringing sessions, not open to the public but lovely to listen to. This church is full of historical artefacts.

The university colleges have produced 18 Archbishops of Canterbury and Cambridge has the highest number of resident clergy per capita in the UK.

## Great St Mary's

To study at Cambridge, it is said that all the undergraduates of the University must live within three miles of The Church of St Mary the Great.

This church is 800 years old and has been designed in a perpendicular style. It is open every day, and Sundays there are church services.

For a fee, it is possible to climb the 123 steps of the bell tower and once you reach the top you will gain a spectacular view of the city.

The Bell Tower of Great St Mary's

A view of King's College from the top of Great St Mary's

## Rowing

There has been rowing on the river Cam since the 1800s. Today in Cambridge there are town rowing clubs, and each university college has its own women's and men's teams. Each morning from as early as 6 am it is possible to find rowers rowing on the river between The Victoria Bridge and Baits Bite Lock. Most months of the year there are events on the river, find them on the Cambridge Rowing Association website. If you would like to row, contact one of the town clubs to enquire if you can book a session.

## HOUSEBOATS AND BOATHOUSES

A 10-minute walk from the city centre will take you to the banks of the River Cam. On the river In between Fort St George pub and the Cutter Ferry Bridge on Midsummer Common, you will find most of the University boathouses and the town rowing clubs. During the weekends or early mornings, you can sit on a bench and watch the rowers training and getting ready to row on the river.

## Swans

Today all swans in the UK belong to the Queen of England. In 1246 Henry III decreed they all belonged to the crown and so it was. Swans are known throughout the world for their strength, fidelity, and grace, and they can fly at speed. According to folklore, swans sing most beautifully before they die and the phrase for a swan song is often used at the final performance of an actor, singer, composer, or poet who leaves the stage in style. References to its use are found in the works of Plato, Aristotle, and Cicero, and Shakespeare used it in several plays. The cygnets and ducklings usually hatch in May and watching and feeding them along the river is a great pastime.

# THE TOUR

Choose where you start and end the tour and begin your day with a relaxing punt or reverse the steps and end with the punt, either way, the tour is fantastic. Scudamore's punting has been working on the River Cam for over 100 years. You will be given a great overview of the city and an unforgettable tour of the local history. Take a picnic and or drinks with you and stylishly enjoy your punt.

# WALKING DIRECTIONS FOR THE TOUR

It is possible to veer off the beaten track and find more of the treasures of Cambridge but if you only have one day, this is the tour for you.

1. Start on Bridge Street, at the punting station next to Magdalene Bridge.
2. Go on a punting tour of the Backs of Cambridge.
3. If you return from the punt and feel peckish, cross over Bridge Street and go into Fitzbillies for coffee and a traditional sticky Chelsea bun.
4. After your coffee, keep on the left and walk away from Magdalene Bridge and the river along Bridge Street towards the town centre.
5. In approximately 3 minutes and 220 yards, you will see The Round Church on your left. This is where you begin the walking tour, take as much or as little time as you need for your journey and stop to take photographs. Visit the places
pointed out in this tour, which gives you a wonderful overview and understanding of Cambridge.

6. With your back to the Round Church, cross the road and walk along St John's Street.

7. Keep to the right of the footpath and take a tour with a guide from St John's College.

8. Come out of St John's, walk further to Trinity College and take a tour of the College if available.

9. St John's Street will change into Kings Parade where you will find King's College.

10. On the left-hand side of the road, you will see on the corner of Benet Street the Corpus Clock.

11. Kings Parade changes into Trumpington Street where you will see 'the other Fitzbillies' coffee shop.

12. Stop in for some refreshments as the next stop is The Fitzwilliam Museum.

13. The Fitzwilliam is found on your right when you continue along Trumpington Street for a further four minutes.

# FAMILY ACTIVITIES AND LINKS

In Cambridge, there is a marvellous array of interesting and educational activities for both adults and children. Activities are held at the local museums, which have too many treasures to write about. If you have time to plan, search the individual websites online and find the times and activities that suit you and your family as many events need to be booked in advance due to the high demand. The Tourist Information Centre has a wealth of knowledge, tours, guides and information. Drop by to plan theatre trips and book tickets to events you want to experience. Below are some links and keywords to search.

Have great fun and learn lots on a great history tour with a difference!https://terribletours.co.uk

Here is the vital link you need to plan an awesome day out in Cambridge for the family https://www.museums.cam.ac.uk/whats-on

The Fitzwilliam Museum https://fitzmuseum.cam.ac.uk/learning/families

The Museum of Zoology https://www.museum.zoo.cam.ac.uk/visit-us/visiting-families

The Polar Museum, Scott Polar Institute https://www.spri.cam.ac.uk/museum/access/

The Botanic Gardens https://www.botanic.cam.ac.uk/whats-on/

Duxford Air Museum In the village of Duxford 10 miles or a short train journey to Whittlesford out of town but well worth a visit particularly if there is a special event on you like WW11 and or aircraft.

https://www.iwm.org.uk/visits/iwm-duxford/whats-o

## History Link

https://opendomesday.org/place/TL4458/cambridge

## Theatre

Cambridge Arts Theatre

An independent theatre in the heart of the city. Find the box office on St Edwards Passage. https://www.cambridgeartstheatre.com

ACD Theatre

Beginning life in 1855 this is the oldest playhouse in Britain. It has a wonderful history with performances originating in the back room of the Hoop Inn. With impressive alumni such as Emma Thompson, Peter Cook, Stephen Fry and Hugh Laurie and Rachel Weisz, this is a theatre to go to.

## Festivals

There are various festivals on the summer calendar in Cambridge. Take a picnic and a blanket to sit on to see a magical performance of Shakespeare in the University College gardens, which are often closed and out of view from the public. https://cambridgeshakespeare.com

## Music

By the river or a recital in the chapels, you will be delighted with the plethora of offerings for a relaxed summer evening out in the city. https://cambridgesummermusic.com/whats-on/

## Night Clubs

Night Clubs for when you want to go out and let your hair down. There are some great places ranging in cost and style. https://ukstudenthouses.com/best-nightclubs-in-cambridge/

## Hidden Gems and Secrets

Cows on the Common! There has been grazing for cows and horses on Midsummer Common since the 12th century. A parliamentary act in 1965 gives people who live or own land in Cambridge permission to graze their animals.

Not being allowed to keep dogs in the student accommodation, it is rumoured that Lord Byron kept a bear instead. Oliver Cromwell was buried in Westminster Abbey in London. However, his skull was dug up and is now buried in Cambridge, can you find out where?

Jesus Green Lido is the longest outdoor swimming pool in Europe.

## Other Bridges and Locks along the Cam

A14 Road Bridge

Abbey Chesterton Bridge

Baits Bite Lock

Coe Fen

Crusoe

Cutter Ferry Bridge

Elizabeth Way Bridge

Fen Causeway

Fort St George Bridge

Green Dragon Bridge

Jesus Lock footbridge

Middle River at Mill Pond

Riverside Bridge. There are plans to rename this bridge the Equiano Bridge after a famous man who lived nearby.

Silver Street

The Railway Bridge

Trumpington Bridge

Victoria Avenue Bridge

None of the recommended places are sponsored but are a selection that combines insider knowledge and what the locals have tried, tested and loved. Check the websites of the recommended places for opening times and costs of extra tours, so you are well planned and can relax and enjoy your day.

# ACKNOWLEDGEMENTS

Hannah Glover and Joseph Lewis for punting us along the backs while Vanessa Champion captured the stunning architecture and life you see in the photographs. Megan Glover for her unwavering encouragement and proofreading. Without these wonderful people, there would be no mini guide to Cambridge, or this useful and easy way to see and experience the wonders of this city.

# REFERENCES

Admin. (2022, January 21). *5 Spots to see the Sunset in Cambridge - Let's Go Punting.* Let's Go Punting. Retrieved August 2, 2022, from https://letsgopunting.co.uk/5-spots-to-see-the-sunset-in-cambridge/

Benoist, J. C. (2016, November, 11). *Churches in Cambridge: an antidote to religious decline.* Varsity Online. Retrieved August 3, 2022, from https://www.varsity.co.uk/culture/11102

Browns. (n.d.). *Afternoon Tea.* Browns Restaurants. Retrieved August 8, 2022, from https://www.browns-restaurants.co.uk/restaurants/eastofengland/cambridge/afternoonteamenu#/

Cambridge Summer Music Ltd. (2022). *Cambridge Summer Music.* Cambridge Summer Music Festival 2022. Retrieved August 3, 2022, from https://cambridgesummermusic.com/whats-on/

Cambridge Walking Tours. (2022). *Punt Cambridge.* Retrieved August 3, 2022, from https://puntcambridge.co.uk/cambridge-walking-tours/

Carreiras, S. (2022, June 27). *Music on the river 2022 is back - Let's Go Punting.* Let's Go Punting. Retrieved August 2, 2022, from https://letsgopunting.co.uk/music-on-the-river-2022/

Cherry, S. (2022). *A Festival of Nine Lessons and Carols.* Kings College Cambridge. Retrieved August 2, 2022, from https://www.kings.cam.ac.uk/chapel/a-festival-of-nine-lessons-and-carols

The Corpus Christi College University of Cambridge. (2022). *An introduction to the Corpus Clock.* Https://Www.Corpus.Cam.Ac.Uk. Retrieved August 2, 2022, from https://www.corpus.cam.ac.uk/about/college/introduction-corpus-clock

Friends of Midsummer Common. (2022). *Grazing on the Common.* Midsummer Common. Retrieved August 3, 2022, from https://midsummercommon.org.uk

granitewordpress. (2022, May 27). *Afternoon Tea in | Clayton Hotel.* The Clayton Hotel. Retrieved August 8, 2022, from https://www.claytonhotelcambridge.com/restaurants-bars/afternoon-tea-cambridge/

Kershman, A. (2020, January 1). *Walking Cambridge: Amazon.co.uk: Andrew Kershman, Sophie Lazar, Hannah Kershman, Hannah Kershman: 9781902910666: Books.* Amazon. Retrieved August 2, 2022, from https://www.amazon.co.uk/Walking-Cambridge-Andrew-Kershman/dp/1902910664/?_encoding=UTF8&pd_rd_w=aptGz&content-id=amzn1.sym.822afc68-e2bb-4420-ac6e-1044cd2e7c1d&pf_rd_p=822afc68-e2bb-4420-ac6e-1044cd2e7c1d&pf_rd_r=9DB6ZX5ZNTFBABCV75JD&pd_rd_wg=Ttb9N&pd_rd_r=4ca63e83-c9fa-43d1-872e-a8c0b2f6d631&ref_=pd_gw_ci_mcx_mi&asin=1902910664&revisionId=&format=4&depth=1

Khan, T. (2021). *10 Things to do in Cambridge.* YouTube.Com. Retrieved August 2, 2022, from https://www.youtube.com/watch?v=j0QpLr1gTXs

Lambert, T. (n.d.). *A History of Cambridge.* Local Histories.

Retrieved August 2, 2022, from https://localhistories.org/a-history-of-cambridge/

Macmichael, S. (2016, December 16). *Cambridge cycle counter logs 1 million trips inside a year.* Road.cc.. Retrieved August 2, 2022, from https://road.cc/content/news/214326-cambridge-cycle-counter-logs-1-million-trips-inside-year

Met Office. (2018, June 15). *Air mass types.* The Met Office. Retrieved
August 2, 2022, from https://www.metoffice.gov.uk/weather/learn-about/weather/atmosphere/air-masses/types

Orchard Tea Garden Limited. (2022, May 19). *Home.* Retrieved August 8, 2022,
from https://www.theorchardteagarden.co.uk

Oxford Summer Courses. (n.d.). *Must watch films set in Cambridge.*
5 Must Watch Films Set in Cambridge. Retrieved August 2, 2022, from https://oxfordsummercourses.com/articles/must-watch-films-set-in-cambridge/

Parkers tavern. (2022, August 8). *Afternoon Tea - Parker's Tavern Brasserie Restaurant, Cambridge.* Parker's Tavern Brasserie Restaurant, Cambridge.
Retrieved August 8, 2022, from https://parkerstavern.com/afternoon-tea/

St Benet's Church. (n.d.). *History of St Benet's Church.* St Benet's Church.
Retrieved August 2, 2022, from https://www.stbenetschurch.org/history

St John's College Cambridge. (2022). *Experience St John's.*
Retrieved August 2, 2022,
from https://www.joh.cam.ac.uk

The Bike Shop Cambridge Station. (2022, January 1). *Bike Shop Cambridge Station | Rutland Cycling.* Retrieved August 2, 2022, from https://www.rutlandcycling.com/store-details/rutland_cycling_cambridge_station_store_detail.html?utm_source=gmblisting&utm_medium=googlesearch&utm_campaign=general

The city of Cambridge: Bridges. (2022). *A History of the County of Cambridge and the Isle of Ely: Volume 3, the City and University of Cambridge.* Ed. J P C Roach. London: Victoria County History, 1959. 114. *British History Online.* Web. Retrieved August 8, 2022. http://www.british-history.ac.uk/vch/cambs/vol3/p114.

The Eagle in Cambridge. (n.d.). *Eagle in Cambridge.* Retrieved August 2, 2022, from https://www.greeneking-pubs.co.uk/pubs/cambridgeshire/eagle/?utm_source=g_places&utm_medium=locations&utm_campaign=

The Fitzwilliam Museum. (2022). *Events.* Retrieved August 3, 2022, from https://fitzmuseum.cam.ac.uk/events

The Stagecoach Bus Company. (2022). *The Stage Coach Bus Company.* Retrieved August 3, 2022, from https://www.stagecoachbus.com/plan-a-journey

The Train Line. (2022). *The Train Line.* The Trainline. Retrieved August 3, 2022, from https://www.thetrainline.com/destinations/trains-to-cambridge
Voi Scooters. (2022). *Voi Scooters.* Retrieved August 3, 2022, from https://www.voiscooters.com

Printed in Great Britain
by Amazon